# Writing Handbook

GRADE
K

Printed in the U.S.A.

ISBN: 978-0-547-86455-6

28 0982 18

4500728616        D E F G

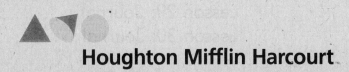

**Houghton Mifflin Harcourt**

# Contents

**Writing Forms** Narrative Writing

Lesson 1: Names. . . . . . . . . . . . . . . . . . . .3
Lesson 2: Labels . . . . . . . . . . . . . . . . . . . 4
Lesson 3: Captions. . . . . . . . . . . . . . . . . .5
Lesson 4: Story Sentences. . . . . . . . . . . 6
Lesson 5: Class Story. . . . . . . . . . . . . . . 7

Informative Writing

Lesson 6: Descriptive Sentences. . . . . . .8
Lesson 7: Descriptive Sentences. . . . . . .9
Lesson 8: Captions. . . . . . . . . . . . . . . . . 10
Lesson 9: Description. . . . . . . . . . . . . . . 11
Lesson 10: Description. . . . . . . . . . . . . . 12

Narrative Writing

Lesson 11: Story Sentences . . . . . . . . . . 13
Lesson 12: Story Sentences. . . . . . . . . . 14
Lesson 13: Story Sentences . . . . . . . . . . 15
Lesson 14: Story . . . . . . . . . . . . . . . . . . 16
Lesson 15: Story . . . . . . . . . . . . . . . . . . 17

Opinion Writing

Lesson 16: Message . . . . . . . . . . . . . . . . 18
Lesson 17: Thank-You Note . . . . . . . . . . 19
Lesson 18: Letter . . . . . . . . . . . . . . . . . 20
Lesson 19: Opinion Sentences . . . . . . . 21
Lesson 20: Opinion Sentences . . . . . . . 22

Informative Writing

Lesson 21: List . . . . . . . . . . . . . . . . . . . 23
Lesson 22: Lists. . . . . . . . . . . . . . . . . . . 24
Lesson 23: Invitation . . . . . . . . . . . . . . . 25
Lesson 24: Report . . . . . . . . . . . . . . . . . 26
Lesson 25: Report . . . . . . . . . . . . . . . . . 27

Opinion Writing

Lesson 26: Response to Literature . . . . . 28
Lesson 27: Response to Literature . . . . . 29
Lesson 28: Response to Literature . . . . . 30
Lesson 29: Journal . . . . . . . . . . . . . . . . . 31
Lesson 30: Journal . . . . . . . . . . . . . . . . . 32

Name _____

# Names

**Teacher:** On the top, have children draw a picture showing themselves and two other children, who can be friends, relatives, or classmates. Below that, have children list the first names of the three people in the picture, one on each set of lines.

Name _____

# Labels

**Teacher:** Have children think about four kinds of animals they like. Ask them to draw one animal in each box. Have children write a label below each drawing that names the kind of animal they drew (deer, puppy, giraffe, etc.).

**4** • Grade K

Name _____

# Captions

**Teacher:** Have children draw a picture showing themselves taking part in a favorite activity. Then have children write a caption to explain what is happening in the picture.

Name _____

# Story Sentences

**Teacher:** Ask children to think of ideas for a made-up character they might like to write a story about. Ask children to draw a picture that shows their character. Then have children write a story sentence to tell more about the picture.

Name _____

# Class Story

**Teacher:** Ask children to choose their favorite part of the class story they just wrote. Have them write about it at the top of the paper. Encourage them to use their own words to tell what happened in that part of the story. Then have them draw a picture to go with the words.

Name _____

# Descriptive Sentences

I chose a _____ .

_____

_____

_____

_____

_____

**Teacher:** Ask children to choose an object from the classroom, draw it, and write its name. Have them write a description of it. Have them use words that describe the way it looks and feels. If appropriate, they can add how it sounds or how it smells, as well. Remind them to write in sentences.

Name _____

# Descriptive Sentences

**Teacher:** Have children draw a picture of a butterfly, a flower, or a fish. Then have children write a descriptive sentence to tell about what they drew.

Name _____

# Captions

Descriptive Sentence

**Teacher:** Have children use color to draw a picture of themselves together with a favorite object, such as a toy, a stuffed animal, a ball, or a book. Then guide them to write a simple caption sentence that uses color or shape words to describe the picture.

Name _____

# Description

My animal has legs.

_____

- - - - - - - - - - - - - - - - - - - - - - - - - -

_____

_____

- - - - - - - - - - - - - - - - - - - - - - - - - -

_____

© Houghton Mifflin Harcourt Publishing Company. All rights reserved.

**Teacher:** Read the sentence at the top of the page as children follow along. Ask children to draw a picture of an animal they like. Have them revise the sentence at the top of the page and write a new sentence at the bottom. The new sentence should use describing words and at least one number word to tell about their animal.

Grade K • 11

Name _____

# Description

Here are some grapes.

_____

- - - - - - - - - - - - - - - - - - - - - - - - - -

_____

- - - - - - - - - - - - - - - - - - - - - - - - - -

_____

**Teacher:** Read the sentence at the top of the page with children. Have them revise the sentence to include information about the size and shape of the grapes. Then have them write the revised sentence at the bottom of the page. Children can color the picture when they are done.

Name _____

# Story Sentences

They ate some food.

---

**Teacher:** Tell children that the sentence at the top of the page comes from a story. Ask children to draw a picture that shows some foods that they especially like to eat. Then ask them to use more exact words to write a new sentence that could also come from a story and names some of the specific foods in the picture.

Name _____

# Story Sentences

<br>

_____
- - - - - - - - - - - - - - - - - - - - -
_____
_____
- - - - - - - - - - - - - - - - - - - - -
_____

**Teacher:** Ask children to think of something fun they would like to do. Have them draw a picture of themselves engaged in this activity. Then have them write a sentence about the picture, using an exact verb.

Name _____

# Story Sentences

A bird was in the tree.

_____

- - - - - - - - - - - - - - - - - - - - - -

_____

_____

- - - - - - - - - - - - - - - - - - - - - -

_____

Then the bird flew away.

**Teacher:** Read the two sentences aloud. Tell children that these sentences are part of a story. Point out that the middle sentence is missing. Ask children to write an appropriate middle sentence that fits with the two existing sentences. Then ask children to draw a picture to illustrate their story.

Name _____

# Story

First, _____ .

Next, _____ .

Last, _____ .

**Teacher:** Have children look at the picture story they created in the previous minilesson. Read the time order words on the page. Ask children to complete the sentence frames by writing what is happening in each picture of the story, being sure to retell the events in the correct order. Offer dictation and spelling help as needed, and encourage children to keep their writing simple and short. Children can draw a picture when their writing is complete.

Name _____

# Story

I saw a dog.

_____

- - - - - - - - - - - - - - - - - - - - - - - - - - - - - -

_____

_____

- - - - - - - - - - - - - - - - - - - - - - - - - - - - - -

_____

**Teacher:** Read the first sentence aloud. Tell children that this sentence is a story idea, but explain that children can revise the sentence to make it better. Ask children to add or change words at the top of the page, then write the complete sentence at the bottom of the page. Finally, ask children to draw a picture to illustrate their story.

Name _____

# Message

_____

- - - - - - - - - - - - - - - - - -

_____

_____

- - - - - - - - - - - - - - - - - - - - - - - - - - - -

_____

_____

- - - - - - - - - - - - - - - - - - - - - - - - - - - -

_____

                                          _____

                                          - - - - - - - - - - - - - - -

                                          _____

**Teacher:** Tell children that they will use this page to write a message to a family member. Help them write the recipient's name at the top and the body of the message below that. Have children end by signing their names and drawing a picture to illustrate the message.

Name _____

# Thank-You Note

_____

- - - - - - - - - - - - - - - - - -

Dear _____,

_____

- - - - - - - - - - - - - - - - - - - - - - - - - - - - -

_____

_____

- - - - - - - - - - - - - - - - -

_____

**Teacher:** Tell children to think of someone who did something nice for them and who they would like to thank. Ask them to write a thank-you note to that person. Assist them in writing the recipient's name at the top and the body of the thank-you note, including reason and opinion, below that. Children should also sign their names and draw a picture.

Name _____

# Letter

Dear _____ ,

Love,

**Teacher:** Have children choose a family member and write a letter to that person. Encourage them to share some interesting news they have.

Name _____

# Opinion Sentences

**Teacher:** Have children choose an animal and draw a picture of it. Then have them write one or two opinion sentences about the animal.

Name _____

# Opinion Sentences

I love to eat fruit.

- - - - - - - - - - - - - - - - - - - - - - - - - - - - - - - - - - - - - - - - - - - - - - - -

- - - - - - - - - - - - - - - - - - - - - - - - - - - - - - - - - - - - - - - - - - - - - - - -

- - - - - - - - - - - - - - - - - - - - - - - - - - - - - - - - - - - - - - - - - - - - - - - -

**Teacher:** Read the first sentence aloud. Remind children that this is an opinion sentence, but tell children that they can revise the sentence to make their opinion clearer. Ask children to use editing symbols to add, delete, or change words at the top of the page, then make a clean copy of the complete sentence at the bottom of the page. Have children draw pictures to illustrate their opinion.

**22** • Grade K

Name _____

# List

# My Favorite Foods

**Teacher:** Ask children to draft a list of their favorite foods. Remind them to put one food on each line. Encourage them to continue their lists on the back of the paper, if needed.

Name _____

# Lists

## Getting Ready for School

_____

- - - - - - - - - - - - - - - - - - - - - - - -

_____

- - - - - - - - - - - - - - - - - - - - - - - -

_____

_____

- - - - - - - - - - - - - - - - - - - - - - - -

_____

- - - - - - - - - - - - - - - - - - - - - - - -

_____

_____

- - - - - - - - - - - - - - - - - - - - - - - -

_____

**Teacher:** Give children the picture lists they created during the previous minilesson. Have them describe the pictures in words and write the list on this page, using numbers for each activity.

Name _____

# Invitation

**Teacher:** Ask children to use the invitation plan they made in Minilesson 45. Have them draft an invitation to a friend or family member based on this plan. They should write *Dear* ___ at the top and their own name at the bottom.

# Report

---

**Teacher:** Give children the papers they completed earlier, in which they noted facts they learned about animals. Guide children to choose 2–3 of these facts and write them in sentence form, then draw a picture.

Name _____

WRITING FORMS

# Report

Cows

Cows eat.

Cows make sounds.

_____
- - - - - - - - - - - - - - - - - - - - - -
_____

_____
- - - - - - - - - - - - - - - - - - - - - -
_____

_____
- - - - - - - - - - - - - - - - - - - - - -
_____

**Teacher:** Read the report on cows aloud. Ask children to revise the report so it is clearer and gives better information. Ask children to write a clean copy of their revision at the bottom of the page and draw a picture.

Name _____

# Response To Literature

_____

- - - - - - - - - - - - - - - - - - - - -

_____

- - - - - - - - - - - - - - - - - - - - -

_____

- - - - - - - - - - - - - - - - - - - - -

_____

- - - - - - - - - - - - - - - - - - - - -

_____

**Teacher:** Display the book you chose. Do a brief picture walk so you're sure the book is familiar to children. Then have children write sentences to respond to the book and draw a picture to go with their response.

Name _____

# Response to Literature

## Realistic Fiction Response

_____
- - - - - - - - - - - - - - - - - - - - - - - -
_____

_____
- - - - - - - - - - - - - - - - - - - - - - - -
_____
- - - - - - - - - - - - - - - - - - - - - - - -
_____
- - - - - - - - - - - - - - - - - - - - - - - -
_____
- - - - - - - - - - - - - - - - - - - - - - - -
_____

**Teacher:** Display a book of realistic fiction and review it with children. Help children copy the title of the book onto the top of the page. Then have children write 2 or more sentences to respond to the story, focusing especially on the realistic parts. Have them close by drawing a picture that goes with their response.

Name _____

# Response to Literature

## Nonfiction Response

**Teacher:** Display a nonfiction book. Review it with children. Have children write the title at the top of the page. Then have children write at least 2 sentences in response to the book, focusing if possible on things they learned. They should draw a picture that goes with their response.

Name _____

# Journal

**Teacher:** Tell children that they will use this page to write and draw a journal entry. Have them write the date at the top of the page. Ask them to think of their favorite part of the school year. Then have them write one or more sentences about that topic and draw a picture.

Name _____

# Journal

**Teacher:** Ask children to write a journal entry on a topic of their choice. They should include the date and a picture. If possible, help them to type their writing on a computer and post it online.